THE SOURCE OF THE DEAL

BY

CHRIS ROOD

D1712911

Ordering Information:
Quantity sales. Special discounts are available on quantity purchases by corporations, associations, and others. Orders by U.S. trade bookstores and wholesalers. Please contact Chris Rood via https://www.ChrisRood.com

Edited and Marketed By
Dream Starters University
www.DreamStartersUniversity.com

Thank you to my wife and five children for supporting me and especially my wife for holding down the fort at home while watching my rug rats, while I work on building our legacy. I love you more then you will ever know.

Table of Contents

Introduction

Ever since I was a kid, I knew that I wanted to be an entrepreneur. It was in my blood. By the time I was in fourth grade I was selling baseball and basketball cards in class. If I knew I had a hot rookie card, then I would sell it for more than what I paid for it, selling the buyer on the fact that it would be worth more in the future. After all, the ability to sell is what makes or breaks an entrepreneur.

Growing up, I always told myself I was going to own a business one day. But I did everything wrong. I had problems staying out of trouble.

I went to a Catholic high school, and I ended up getting my girlfriend (who is now my wife) pregnant when I was 17 years old. Needless to say, this was not acceptable at a Catholic school and I was looked down upon, which had an effect on the way I thought about myself for some time.

In my late teens and early twenties, I messed around with drugs and got caught up with the wrong crowd partying every weekend and making a lot of bad choices. At 22, I realized I needed to get my shit together or else my life was going to get out of control fast.

So I checked myself into a program to help me clean my body of all the drugs and toxins I had put into it. I also did a deep dive into personal development books. I took courses on bettering myself and really focused on self-improvement.

Three months later while in college I started my own business doing on-site oil changes and car washes out of the back of my truck. By the time I was a senior in college, I was making almost 100k a year.

By the time I graduated college, I was pretty pumped about my oil change business because all of my buddies who were looking for jobs were landing jobs right out of college for 30k a year, and I was making 6 figures already at graduation. So I decided to keep doing what I was doing after college to grow my business even more.

Two years later, right after Hurricane Katrina hit New Orleans, there was a huge influx people that were moving from New Orleans to the Baton Rouge, Lafayette and Houston areas because they were displaced by the hurricane. This influx of people drove real estate prices through the roof. High demand and low inventory in my area made my house almost double in value overnight.

I recognized this opportunity and decided to fix up my house and put it up for sale. Two months later I sold it and made 125k! I invested that money into my first quick-lube/mechanic's shop. I didn't have to do on-site anymore. Customers would have to come to me!

We then got another lucky break and were able to buy a pre-foreclosure in a good neighborhood. We decided to move into it and fix it up. Two years later, I flipped this house and used the money to buy another shop.

Having my own shops allowed me to focus even more on my work. Because the business was doing so well, I decided to focus on my shops, and by the time I was 26 I was making $350,000 a year and had around 30 employees.

I was doing so well, I basically put real estate on the backburner. Life was good, but I was working extremely hard to keep everything running. I was trading time for money.

A couple of years later, I decided I wanted to invest some of the cash I was making into real estate to keep my money working for me, so I bought around 3 million dollars' worth of single-family homes off of MLS for around 75-80 cents on the dollar. I made good cash flow from these properties for a couple of years until the bottom fell out of the oil and gas industry in 2014. The price of oil went from $120 a barrel to $28 a barrel. We lost thousands of jobs in my area. It devastated my area economically.

My shops lost 40-50% in sales in less than a year. My rental properties went vacant because I had bought too high and bought too many higher end rentals.

Right around the same time this was happening, I came across the concept of wholesaling real estate. I had no idea what it was at the time, but I researched it a lot online to try to figure out how it worked. After learning the basics on my own, I wholesaled a few properties, and I made 5 to 15k here and there, but it was very inconsistent. To really get an understanding of it, I hired three mentors back to back to back. Doing this helped me to put all the pieces together, and a few months later I made 47k in one month.

It was perfect timing for me because my other businesses were not doing well with the economy making a correction where I lived.

I did so well from there on out that I went to work for two of my mentors in their sales department, and another mentor asked me to develop a course with him on some of the strategies I was implementing in my market.

Long story short, one of my mentors ended up stealing 50k from me by having my credit card on file and deceiving me into partnering with him. Eight months later, I had him arrested and the money returned. Never the less, while I was doing sales for some of my mentors, I began to take note of the students who were successful and those who weren't.

Before long, I realized I could spot the reasons why people were failing, and I could spot the reasons why others were succeeding. These were things I felt I needed to share.

At this point, I had a light bulb moment. I realized I was actually a better wholesaler than my coach. I was doing more deals than they were, and so I decided it was time to go out on my own to help other people. Since then, I've had so many students working in real estate tell me, "Man, thank you. You turned my whole business around."

Wholesaling real estate was a total game changer for me! Wholesaling teaches you how to find deals. This is where you should start if you want to get into real estate. Why? Because it shows you how to become the source of the deal.

It puts you in first position in capturing equity on properties. If you don't learn how to buy right, you'll fail fast! What's every investor looking for? A good what? A good DEAL! This is what wholesaling real estate creates!

It creates a pipeline of motivated seller leads for you to pick from. Once you're the source of the deal, you can cherry pick from the pipeline of deals to wholesale, flip, wholetail, or buy and hold.

Don't make the same mistake I made by not starting with wholesaling. If I had started with wholesaling, I would have gotten 10X better deals than the ones I bought on MLS. I literally buy deals now for 30-60 cents on the dollar because I know the marketing strategies required to do so.

With this book, I'm going to show you exactly what I teach my students and how and why it all works. Most importantly, I'm going to teach you how to become ***THE SOURCE OF THE DEAL***.

Don't just play the game. Learn to dominate like I have! Let's get started!

Chapter 1

What is Real Estate Wholesaling?

I'm not like most real estate wholesaling coaches. I teach a slightly different marketing strategy to my students. I give my students a step-by-step process to follow, and it's the exact process I used to get started in this business. In fact, I still use it to this day.

But let's back up and get a clear definition of what it means to be a real estate wholesaler in the first place. A real estate wholesaler is someone who markets to motivated sellers using a variety of marketing strategies and then contracts a property heavily discounted at, say, 60 cents on the dollar or less. Then he or she markets "an assignable contract" to a cash buyer or an investor for what is called an assignment fee, which could be 5-20k or more. The assignment fee is paid by the buyer and kept by the wholesaler.

Alternatively, if you have cash available to buy a property yourself, you can close on it yourself, and then turn around and sell it to an investor for more. This is how you can keep buyers and sellers from knowing how much money you're making. This is called a double close.

There is also a way to not show how much money you're making if you don't have the money to double close. It's called a seller side only HUD statement, and it hides what you're making on a property when you assign a contract from the seller. Without doing this, sellers can figure out on their own how much money you're making on a deal when you sell the assignment contract.

Now, understand that not all these strategies are applicable in every state. You can do these methods in most states. However, there are a few states that are not wholesale friendly. Check your local state laws.

Sometimes buyers will also get upset about how much money you're making. But, ideally, they aren't going to care because the idea is to leave them enough equity in the property that even when you make money, they still get a good deal, so they can make even more money.

As you build relationships with investors who want to invest in the deals you've found for them, they should be okay with you making money for doing all the work of finding and putting a deal together for them. However, there are some strategies I go over in my wholesaling course for how to deal with this that I don't have enough time to go over in this book.

Being a real estate wholesaler is kind of like being the Amazon of real estate. Amazon has sellers who they contract with, and they put those sellers' products on their website. Then they charge a fee to those sellers for each product sold, and that's one of the ways Amazon makes money. The difference in wholesaling real estate is that the fee is ultimately charged to the buyer using an assignable contract, not the original homeowner. The other difference is you're marketing a contract, not a property.

Wholesaling is a fantastic business model to get into in real estate because anyone can do it. Wait! I don't want to mislead you, because not everyone can be successful in this business. You need a certain skill set. "Skills get the deals" is what I always tell my students, but that's a topic for another time. (Go watch the interview I did with Grant Cardone on YouTube where I cover this.)

What I mean to tell you is you don't have to have a real estate license to get started. You don't have to have millions or even hundreds of thousands of dollars to get started. You don't have to have a bunch of money to invest in buying properties yourself. You just have to connect motivated sellers to hungry cash buyers, and this book is going to show you exactly how to do that.

Skills Get the Deals

A real estate wholesaler is someone who markets to motivated sellers using a variety of marketing strategies. They then contract a property heavily discounted, and they market an assignable contract to an investor for an assignment fee, which they keep as payment for finding the deal. You don't have to have a real estate license or lot of money to get into this business. You just have to connect motivated sellers to cash buyers. This book will show you how.

Chapter 2

Problems = Motivation = DEALS

As a real estate wholesaler, your job is to market to people with problems. So as your marketing goes out, and the leads come in, your job is to filter through them by listening and asking the right questions to find the motivation.

You have to learn to listen for motivation, a skill I help you develop in my coaching program. If a seller doesn't have a problem in their life, they're not going to sell to you heavily discounted, PERIOD!

You can't force motivation. Either a seller is motivated, or they're not. If they're not, move on. It's a numbers game in this business. You'll hear X amount of no's before you finally get to that yes! You have to learn to get through the no's without getting frustrated, wanting to quit or getting butt hurt about it. It's all a part of the process.

The key is to listen and ask the right questions to find the problem. You want to ask strategic questions like: Why are you trying to sell your house? How fast do you need to sell it? Where are you moving to? How much time do you need to move out?

If you ask enough of the right questions, you will get to the source of why they are selling, which will be the problem that creates the motivation, which creates the DEAL!

Nobody is going to sell you their house for 60 cents on the dollar or less if they don't have a major problem in their life. If they don't need things to move fast, they typically don't have a problem, and they can just sell their home with a realtor and get the full retail price for it.

The people you are looking for are motivated sellers, people with problems! They could be anybody! They could be a burned out landlord. They could be someone whose home is in pre-foreclosure. They could be someone who inherited a property that has become a financial burden, or someone who has lost a job or got a job transfer and needs to sell their house quickly.

They could be anyone who is in distress or has made a bad financial decision that has made it so they need to sell their home for whatever they can get for it, as fast as they can, just to stay afloat.

You get my drift… The point is problems = motivation = deals. This is where the deals are!

18

Skills Get the Deals

Your job as a real estate wholesaler is to market to motivated sellers. People with problems are the only ones who will be motivated to sell at a discount. If there is no motivation, move on. This is a numbers game. Problems = motivation = deals!

Chapter 3

Marketing to Sellers

Every successful business starts with a successful marketing strategy. My marketing strategy will be different than yours, meaning what works in my market will not necessarily work in your market.

People ask me all the time, "What's your secret marketing formula?" The secret is... there is no secret! You have to figure out what works in your market.

You have to split test, measure, adapt, and change your marketing strategy depending on the market you're in. Essentially, you have to learn your market.

The only way to do this is to spend money on different marketing channels, and then track and measure the results you get. I crush it with bandit signs, but I know a lot of wholesalers that have no luck with them.

I don't do a whole lot of direct mail because it hasn't generated a good response for me. However, I know other wholesalers who are crushing it with direct mail. I crush it with online marketing, but I know people who haven't had any luck with it.

It's the same for cold calling. I know people killing it with cold calling, but I'm not a big cold calling fan. I know it works, but I think it's too much work, and I don't want to manage a huge cold calling office and try to keep 3-4 people motivated to make 60-100 calls a day.

I always tell my students, "I don't want to chase motivation… I want motivation to chase me!" Meaning, I'd rather have motivated sellers trying to find me because they need my service.

The best way to explain this is to think about being a hunter trying to hunt deer. If I were hunting deer, I wouldn't want to just go wandering around the woods looking for a deer to shoot. I would want to set up some bait, let's say some corn in the middle of a field, and then I would wait for the deer to come find me!

The same is true for sellers. Why? Because if they are looking for me, I know they're motivated to sell their house to me. They have essentially qualified themselves once they've found me because they have seen my advertisement, which could be my PPC ad or a bandit sign.

They know we buy houses fast for cash, and they know we are not retail buyers by the way our ad communicates to them. They could have called a realtor, but, no, they called us. Why? Because typically these types of people are in distress or have some type of problem in their lives, and they need a quick sale. This means they are willing to trade out equity in order for us to save them time.

When it comes to chasing motivation versus motivation chasing you, I like to compare it to a sniper approach versus a shotgun approach. You can set up some really targeted marketing like PPC, SEO, Facebooks ads, bandit signs or a newspaper article, etc. This is a sniper approach because you're putting out the "corn" in a very strategic place, and then you're waiting for motivated sellers to come to you.

The shotgun approach is where you are shooting in every random direction, as in mailing 5,000 people at one time or cold calling a list of 2,000 people hoping to hit something. Now, I'm not saying you can't get deals this way. You can. Especially if you're hitting an untapped, niche list that no one has exhausted yet.

However, this is why most people fail at wholesaling. Most coaches are telling all their students to mail the same lists that every other guru is telling their students to mail. Then what happens is the students get no response and run out of marketing money because the list they are mailing to has been mailed to 100 times already.

Furthermore, when you're mailing that many people or cold calling that many people, it's a lot of work to manage all the incoming calls if you don't have a team or you're not prepared for it. All the calls can become overwhelming because 98% of the ones that will come in will not be from motivated sellers.

A lot of the calls coming in will be people calling you to tell you to kick rocks and never contact them again. I've even had the cops called on me many times.

The point is if you're a newbie investor looking to get into wholesaling or a seasoned investor just looking for more deals to buy, I suggest you go with the sniper approach when it comes to your marketing campaign so that you don't wear yourself out with all the unmotivated people calling you for no reason.

If you take the shotgun approach, you will need to set up a team to take all the calls, and you will have to manage them all. The sniper approach is way less work!

You get a fraction of the calls coming in. However, the calls that do come in are typically from people who are way more motivated to sell.

They're chasing you! So, these sellers have a way different mindset. To put it simply, when they are chasing you, they are way better quality leads. Please note: There's a chart at the end of this book that shows you different marketing channels and which ones to use or not use in relation to how much time and money you have available.

Skills Get the Deals

You don't want to chase motivation. You want motivation to chase you! If you're a newbie just getting started in wholesaling, go with the targeted, sniper approach to marketing. It's less work, and it produces better quality leads. The shotgun approach can work, but you will talk to many unqualified leads and waste a lot of time, effort and money.

Chapter 4

Bragging to Branding

Imagine you're at a restaurant. You're waiting for your food, and you get bored. The conversation at the table is at a lull.

What's the first thing you do? You pull out your phone, and you start scrolling. You could run this scenario through in any number of ways. But the fact is that in this day and age, when people have spare time to kill, they kill it by looking at their phone. What this means for you if you're in business is that you want to put yourself where people's eyes are—online. Furthermore, if you have an online presence, you seem more credible, and you look like a true business.

If you're in business, you want to be extremely active on social media. You also want to have your website up and running, because that's where everyone is going to look to find out more about you. If they can't get your information easily online, they're going to move on and do business with somebody else who is more accessible.

In my business, we make $60,000 in revenue on a slow month. On a good month, we reach $120,000 in revenue. So where is all this money coming from? Well, 50% of my business comes from online marketing done through SEO, Google AdWords, and Facebook ads.

I call this the trifecta. Why? Because if you're using all three of these strategies, you'll become omnipresent, meaning, you'll be everywhere! In addition to that, you will get your website ranking number one fast in your area because you'll have so much traffic being directed to your website via SEO, Google AdWords and Facebook ads. All this action being directed to your site will tell Google that you're popular and relevant, which means Google will shoot your website up the rankings fast.

But before you get to using those strategies as a real estate wholesaler, there's another free strategy you can use online to build your business without spending a dime. I call it "the bragging to branding strategy."

This is a very simple strategy, but it really works. The essence of the strategy is using social media to tell everybody what you do, how you do it, and how good you are at it, so that your business can grow organically. You want to leverage your social media account so everybody knows who you are.

For example, if you live near me, you know who I am and what I do. Why? Because I'm all over social media. People connected to me in my area see all my Facebook traffic. They see that I'm constantly doing business with different people, and that I have a steady stream of happy customers.

When I have a happy customer, I do a Facebook live with them for my audience. I talk with them about the process we went through, and we talk about how I was able to help them get out of the crisis situation they were in with their home. I get them to "brag" about me to my audience.

When your customers speak for you, that's powerful because it shows other people that you are the real deal. It shows that you care, and that you aren't a flake. It shows that you actually do what you say you do, and that you can be trusted.

Giving your customers the opportunity to tell more people about what you do is a great way to grow your brand and business without having to spend money. It still requires work, and it requires you to put yourself out there, but the benefits are huge.

If you just talk about yourself and how great you are all the time on social media, that starts to come off the wrong way. But when you allow your customers to talk about you and tell other people how great you are, that means something to people.

When you do enough of these live videos, over time your brand starts to become recognized by others. What I do with the videos I make is I take them, and I put them in different area community groups on Facebook. Almost every area has these kinds of local groups, and a quick search on Facebook for your city name will likely turn them up.

I post my videos in the different community groups in my area not to make a direct sale necessarily. My strategy is just to get people to know my brand. Because the people who look at these videos might not be the ones who need to sell their property fast, but they might know someone—their uncle, their brother, whoever—that does need to sell, and they'll tag them in the comments.

I've found that a lot of people want to make marketing a very complicated concept. But the truth is people just need to know who you are, what you do, and that you do it well. When you can show people these three things in any way, then you can increase your sales organically without having to spend money, by leveraging social media.

You don't have to do all of your organic outreach online, either. I always have my business cards on me wherever I go. I talk about my business with everyone, and I'm always telling people what I do and how I do it.

When I'm at the soccer field watching my kids play, I talk to people. I tell them I buy houses and rental property. I've made it a habit of mine just to let people know what I do. I've found that most people are genuinely interested in helping me out if they can. But if they don't know what I do, how can they help me?

I've also made it a habit of networking with people who are in the game. Realtors are in the game. They know all the motivated sellers. They know the people who are having problems and need to sell their properties quickly.

I don't want to miss out on any opportunity, so I've gotten to know all the realtors in my town. Many of them I work out with at the gym, and every single day I go in there to work out I ask them, "Where's the deals?"

I want to be the very first person they think of whenever a deal pops up, so I remind them every day that I'm the guy they need to talk to if they want to get things moving fast. I want the name ~~Chris Rood~~ *Dan Couture* to be branded into their minds. When they know someone that needs to sell their house, I want them to think ~~Chris Rood~~. *Dan Couture*

When you do all of these things, the results are sometimes not immediate. But they have a compounding effect. When you can combine all of these organic strategies with paid advertising, then you are truly maximizing your marketing and branding efforts.

Skills Get the Deals

To brand yourself in your market, you need to let people know you who are you, what you do and how good you are at it. One of the best ways to do this is online through social media. You want to put yourself out there, but it's also important to get your customers to talk about the experience they had with you. Get them to tell everyone what great work you do and how you've helped them, and slowly you will begin to get more leads, make more sales and grow your business. Network with people in your area who are involved in real estate and those who aren't. You never know where your next lead might come from.

Chapter 5

Relationships Are Everything

If you are just getting started wholesaling real estate, and you don't have a $10,000 marketing budget, which most people don't, you have to become very good at building relationships. You have to learn to network with the people who are in the trenches and know what's going on with homeowners in your area. The people you obviously want to get to know in your area are the realtors!

The less obvious people you want to get to know are the mailmen, firefighters, cops, bail bondsmen, divorce attorneys, property managers, assisted living owners and workers, and contractors. Believe it or not, these people might be able to give you a lead.

Let's take a quick look at how your mailman might be able to help you. Mailmen are always putting out the mail at people's houses, so they know when something weird is going on at a house. They know when people are no longer even checking their mail or cutting their grass. When people are no longer checking their mail or cutting their grass, that's generally a sign they are having some kind of problem (Remember from chapter two: problems = motivation = deals).

It might seem unorthodox, but if you tell your mailman you'll give him a couple hundred bucks for every house he sends you that looks distressed that you close on, he'll constantly try to help you. He doesn't really have to do any extra work. All he has to do is keep an eye out for anything weird going on, so it's a win-win situation for both of you!

Firefighters and cops can also help you. They're the first people at the scene of a fire or crime scene. These people are around who? People with problems!

The big key takeaway is you need to connect with people! The more people you talk to, the more money you'll make, period! Almost everyone can help you in some way because everyone has different connections that might know valuable information about people who need to sell their house fast!

This is especially true if you live in a small town that you were born and raised in where everybody knows everyone. Going back to the last chapter on branding, tell everyone what you do and how you do it! Why not use what other people know to your advantage to create free leads for yourself?

Get to know everyone in your area related to real estate and the people I mentioned. I call this relationship marketing, and it's the perfect way to get started if you're just getting started with a low marketing budget. All you need is some cards with your business name and number on them. We get tons of deals every year from people just like this as a result of my team and I networking.

Now let's talk about the flip side of this. Once you get these great deals, who are you going to sell them to? Well, if you have enough money you can buy them off of ListSource.com or from another list company. But if you're like most newbie wholesalers, you probably don't have a whole lot of cash to do this, and you'll need to do things the old-fashioned way through networking.

You can find people in your town who have cash and want your deals. They don't necessarily have to be people who are already in real estate for you to get them to want your deals. You just have to have confidence in yourself, your deals and your ability to get the investor to see the value in the opportunity of investing in your deal. The way you do that is by selling him or her on it.

Right now, banks are giving less than 1% interest on money that's sitting in the bank. So for people who've got $1 million just sitting in the bank, they're only earning $10,000 a year on their money. That's a terrible return, right?

I can take that $1 million and help them buy heavily discounted properties for, say, 50-70% on the dollar. So let's say I helped my investor buy some 30-50k homes worth 60-80k that average $750-850 a month in rent.

With $1 million, I could help my investor buy around 20-33 houses that cash flow around $750-850 a month. That would mean the investor would make around 204k-297k annually on the $1 million sitting in those houses spitting out cash flow!

So when you show people that have cash in the bank or other business owners who have cash these kinds of numbers, they tend to want to work with you. If you can find them single-family homes to invest in for 50-70% on the dollar, their decision should be a no-brainer.

What I do, and what you should do is show them how buying your deal with lots of equity can lead to them earning serious cash flow every month versus their money sitting in the bank. In my town I've created a lot of investors to add to my list by showing them exactly how much money they can make when they work with me using the illustration above.

The advantage to creating investors to add to your list is that newer investors are way more willing to be more aggressive when buying your deals versus seasoned real estate investors that will nickel and dime you to death so that you don't make money off of them.

The best thing to do is sell to newer investors first to maximize profits. The more seasoned the investor, the greedier they will be. Remember this when selling your deals!

In addition, landlord investors will pay you way more for your deals versus rehabbers and flippers! I try to focus on selling my deals to landlords first and flippers last. Remember this also!

Now, if you want to just go find a bunch of investors fast, my favorite way is using bandit signs with ghost ads on them that say "Investor Special 3-2 75k Cash Only" with your cell phone number underneath. You'll have tons of investors calling you.

A couple of other good ways to buy a buyers list fast is at REI meetups, section 8 offices, and sheriff auction sales. Just remember these guys will be seasoned vets and will try every which way to steal the deal from you. Hold your own, and don't let them take advantage of you and your deals. It's got to be win-win for both of you.

One thing that's incredibly important for me to mention is that when you're doing this, you have to make sure you're not "marketing a property." You have to be doing what's called an assignment. In other words, you have to be marketing an assignable contract for a fee. This is how you can be in this business without having to have some sort of license.

What I came to realize after being in the real estate wholesaling business for a while was that I was giving my deals away. I wasn't making much money because I was selling a lot of my deals to flippers. If you want to make the most money you possibly can in this business, take this piece of advice to heart: don't sell your deals to flippers unless you have to. Instead, focus on selling your deals to investors who are or want to be landlords. Landlords will pay you way more money. I wanted to mention this again because it's very important.

Why is this the case? Well, flippers have to get a deal for very cheap so they can be profitable themselves. They need to make money by putting the property back on the market at a higher price, so they have to get it at very low price from the start for it to be worth it for them to buy it from you.

Landlords are willing to pay more money because they're not looking to flip properties for fast cash. Because landlords are looking for cash flow over time as I mentioned earlier, they don't have to rehab the whole property. They don't have to make it perfect in order to sell it like flippers often do. They just have to make sure it's in good enough shape to rent.

So, I've built relationships with all the landlords in my town. The landlords are the first guys I talk to when I've got a new deal, not the flippers. Flippers are an option of last resort. If no landlords want to buy your deal, then you move on to the flippers.

Once I started operating this way, that's when my business exploded. My assignment fees doubled, and I started making a lot more money even though I was doing the same amount of deals each month. An understanding of how this business really works makes a huge difference in how profitable you can become with it. That's why I've written this book to help people who want to be successful real estate wholesalers.

It doesn't matter what part of this business you're talking about, whether its marketing to bring in potential leads or talking with potential investors, you have to know how to build relationships with people. If you aren't someone who is comfortable with talking to other people and negotiating with them, then this business isn't for you. But if you've got energy, passion and drive, and you love to talk to people and help them as they help you, then the sky is truly the limit.

Skills Get the Deals

Doing well in this business all comes down to being able to build relationships. Everyone in your community could potentially give you a lead on your next deal. Once you've got a deal, do your best to sell it to a landlord first. If you can't sell it to a landlord, then sell it to a flipper. But landlords will generally be willing to pay more, so I always start with them first. If you don't know any landlords in your area, but you do know people who are sitting on a lot of cash, talk to them about the advantages of investing in real estate for the purpose renting it out. If you can sell them on the idea of your deals, then you can build a mutually beneficial relationship that will help you both make more money together for a long time.

Chapter 6

Don't Get Too Close

When you're wholesaling real estate, don't get too close to your investors. Always remember they're in it for the deals. If you let them into your space, and they become your friend, they're going to try to take advantage of you.

They're going to try to figure out how you're doing what you're doing. They're going to try figure out how you got the deal you're selling them, and then they're going to try to force you to give it to them for cheaper.

You want to have great business relationships with your investors, and you want to communicate well with them, but don't let them into your inner circle. This keeps them in mystery about you and your deals.

When somebody doesn't know how you get your deals, they gravitate towards you more. But if you chase your investors, they're going to think your deals aren't all that great. They're going to think you're desperate to make a sale.

There was one particular investor who tried to get in my space and figure out how I get my deals. He wanted to be my friend, but only because he wanted to start his own business in my market.

I think what happened was I got careless, and I let him know upfront what I was making on our deals together. I was making $40,0000 off of him a month, and he got jealous. He wanted to do what I was doing, so he started to steal my exact process.

But I caught him. He was paying somebody to pull my bandit signs down and put his down right where mine were. I called him out on it.

We quit talking for a little while, and I backed away from him. But I still sell my deals to him when it works out, but I'm just not as close to him as I was.

However, I learned a valuable lesson from all of this I will never forget: money makes people do strange things. I should have recognized this sooner. Back when we were close, he always wanted to know what I got the deal for and how much I was making, and I would tell him.

Now I always teach my students how to avoid this situation. If someone asks you for this information, don't give it to them upfront. It's none of their business how much you're making. When they ask you, just ask them right back, "Is the price good for you?"

That's what they need to be focused on, because it's the only thing that makes sense for you to talk about with them. If the deal makes good sense for them to take, then they should take it and not worry about what you're making off of the deal.

In sales, it's all about what your customer stands to gain. The conversation should never be about you and what you stand to gain or lose. People who are buying from you don't care about that. They care about themselves. When you take this approach, you will protect yourself.

Enthusiasm mixed with confidence will help you sell your deals. If you're enthusiastic about what you're selling, the person you're selling to is going to feel that. They're going to think, "Man, I want to buy from this guy. This sounds like a really good deal."

You have to have good intentions when you're selling. For me personally, I never want to sell somebody anything that they don't need. For every deal I make, I want to show my intention is to sell something to someone because they need it, it's a great product, and I believe in it.

So, you don't want to get too close to investors you're doing business with. But you still want to surround yourself with the right people who are out there doing big things in business.

You've probably heard the saying that you are the average of your five closest friends, and that your income is the average of your five closest friends. I talk about this all the time because it really is true. You want to be friends with people who are successful, and you want to be around people who are actually trying to make themselves and the world a better place.

Me personally, I don't do anything unless it's something with my wife and kids, something related to personal development, or something related to business. I don't go hang out and drink beer and watch football. Because every time I do, I end up asking myself why I'm even there in the first place. If something doesn't produce an end result that benefits myself or the people I care about, then I don't want any part of it.

If you want to be extremely successful, you have to become obsessed with your business. I've gotten to where I am today because I am obsessed with becoming a better version of myself, helping my family and helping other people get to my level.

Skills Get the Deals

Be careful of who you spend your time with. Don't get too close with your investors. Don't tell them upfront how much money you're making, or they may get jealous and stop doing deals with you or try to become your competitor. Conversely, you want to network with other like-minded people who are doing big things. Find people who can motivate you to improve, and stick with them. Don't waste your time. Obsess over what's important.

Chapter 7

The Recession Proof Business

I used to sell my deals to people who were always asking me to sell them for cheaper than I really wanted to. It got to the point where I was making hardly any money at all. But then I came across people who were more interested in long-term cash flow, and I realized that they always responded positively to the deal I presented them with. They never tried to bring me down in price.

These people are typically landlords, as I explained in the previous chapter. Landlords that you want to sell to are typically going to be in their 30s or 40s, because it's around this time in life that people start to invest in properties to rent out for the duration of their retirement.

Once a landord gets into their 50s, they're typically not buying anymore properties. The reason being that they usually already own as many properties as they want to, and they are at the point in life where they just want to sit on their cash flow.

However, sometimes you can get a good deal from a burned out landlord who doesn't want to or, for whatever reason, can't maintain ownership of their property any longer. In fact, this is the best time in history to be a real estate wholesaler because the baby boomer generation was the biggest demographic in world history. They're all retiring right now, and lots of them own real estate.

The average family back in the baby boom generation had 8 to 10 kids. This was the post World War II generation. When they got back from the war, they had a lot of children because everyone farmed. They needed lots of hands to work the farm.

According to AARP, 10,000 baby boomers are reaching retirement age every single day. And just beyond that, they are going into nursing homes for care and passing away, leaving behind properties to their kids. Many of these aging baby boomers own single-family homes and rental properties, so there's a huge transfer of wealth that's occurring right now in the United States.

What this means for real estate wholesalers is there's a huge influx of supply that's happening, so this equates to more deals to be had. The homes that boomers are leaving behind are generally outdated. When a family inherits a home like this, they know they can't get full retail for it in most cases, so they are willing to sell it for a good price.

I buy deals that are inherited houses often, because a lot of times when kids inherit their parents' house, they just want to get rid of it. They don't want to go through all the hassle of updating it and selling it through a realtor.

So, when you look at the big picture, you can see that this is one of the best times ever in history to be in real estate. Most people don't realize that there's going to be a huge wealth transfer as the baby boomers leave behind their properties, which is exactly why you need to get in on it.

Real estate wholesaling is recession-proof because if the economy crashes, this means there's going to be more deals to be had. More problems are going to occur for people. And as you now know: problems = motivation = deals. I love real estate wholesaling because it thrives in a down economy. It's the perfect all-weather business.

In Lafayette, Louisiana where I live, we just went through the oil and gas bust of 2014. Oil went from being as high as $110 a barrel to being as low as $28 a barrel. We lost thousands of jobs in this area. But this created opportunity for me because it meant people had to downsize their homes. Many people were faced with the reality that they either had to sell their home or go into foreclosure.

In a super-hot market, it's tough to make money wholesaling. It's tough to get deals because people don't have to sell their homes for any lower than retail value. Sometimes they can even sell their homes for more than what they're probably worth because of all the buyers in competition with each other. This is happening in super-hot markets like Miami, Florida and Denver, Colorado.

In hot markets, houses are sold within weeks for above asking price. If you want to get deals in those markets, you have to work a lot harder because deals are scarce.

I tell my students all the time, "Look, if you're having troubles right now, hang tight. Learn how to find discounted properties and how to wholesale, and the right timing will come for you." The problem is most people think when markets are hot and prices are high, they're always going to be that way. And they think that when markets are cold and prices are low, they're always going to be that way, too.

But markets are cyclical. So if you're in a market that is booming right now, you want to be selling as much as possible. But if you're in a down market, you want to go all in and get as many properties under contract as you can, because eventually prices are going to go up again. You've got to ride the waves.

It takes courage to do this. You have to be able to see value, equity and opportunities. The name of the game is buying low and selling high. To do that, you have to take some chances. You have to take some risk. But if you're willing to do that, the rewards can be immense.

The point is the worse the economy gets, the better your wholesaling business will get. This doesn't mean you will not get any deals in a hot market. It just means you'll have to work harder and spend more on marketing, and your closing skills and follow up game will have to be sharper than most.

Skills Get the Deals

Right now, a huge transfer of wealth is occurring because baby boomers are moving out of their homes or leaving them behind to family members. Most of the time, these homes are out of date. The family can't get full retail for them, and often they want to sell them fast. This means it's a great time to get into real estate wholesaling because there's going to be an influx of properties available for low prices. Additionally, all markets move in cycles of boom and bust. When markets are booming, prices are high. This is the time when you want to be selling. When markets are down, this is when you want to be buying because this is when you will get the best deals.

Chapter 8

Become the Source of the Deal

In this business, not only do you have to sell yourself to the homeowner, you also have to sell yourself to the investor. You've got to make the deal look attractive. If you don't know your numbers, you're never going to get an investor to buy your deal.

Investors are smart. They're the ones with the money, and most of the time they got that money by knowing what they're doing when it comes to business. So you have to be knowledgeable about what you're offering them. You have to sell them on the benefits and advantages of buying your deal versus putting their money to use elsewhere. It's a process of negotiation.

You need to come prepared to the negotiation with facts about why it's in the best interest of the investor to take the deal. You've got to know facts about the property like the school district its in, the average rent for the area and the value that other properties in the area are holding.

If you have a property manager you can hook them up with to manage the property for them after they buy it, bring that to the table. Make it easy for them to say yes. Do everything in your power to make your offer as appealing as possible.

It's all about confidence. You have to be so confident about your deal , that even if you can't afford the deal yourself, you want to buy it. If your not confident about your deal your investor will not be either, especially if he is a new investor.

One of the reasons I've been able to become so successful is because I was a landlord before I became a professional wholesaler. Because of my experience in real estate, I know what landlords want. I know what's in their best interest, and I know what they're looking for out of a deal. I suggest to all my students that they become familiar with every aspect of the real estate business in order to become the best wholesaler they can possibly become

When you become the source of the deal, you can branch out into working in all the different facets of real estate if you want to. If you choose to and you have the skills, you can flip the homes you get under contract. Also, if you want to start building cash flow for retirement, you can keep them and become a landlord. If you don't want to do those things, you can still make a lot of money selling contracts for assignment fees.

This is the amazing thing about this business. You have options. There is limitless room for growth, and if you get tired of running your business a certain way, you can pivot and change things up quite easily. This is why you must be knowledgeable about all areas of real estate, because they can all be used to your benefit when you're the source of the deal.

This is what makes this business model so powerful. You become the source of the deal once you have a wholesaling business set up and generating leads from motivated sellers every day. Having this set up gives you the advantage of being in first position on the deals so you capture the most equity.

From there, you can do whatever you want with the deal. You can wholesale, flip, wholetail or keep it in your portfolio. Either way you're in the best situation because you control the deal. If you were to start out as an investor without having a wholesale business, and you bought deals from another wholesaler, you would lose 5-30k or more per deal by not having your own wholesale business set up. But when you become the wholesaler, you take away that middleman, and you become THE SOURCE OF THE DEAL!

It's not easy to be the source of the deal. It requires you to use a specific set of skills that not everyone has. To be a successful wholesaler, you have to have a lot of patience. Sometimes you have to act as a psychologist for people and really listen to them tell you about their problems when they're going through very difficult times. You have to sit down with people sometimes for hours, and you have to help them work through how they're going to get out of the situation they're in.

I can't tell you how many times I've dealt with people who are incredibly difficult and unpredictable. I've had to give money and support to a girl who was addicted to meth. She couldn't feed and clothe her baby because she was losing her house. So I had to go and meet her at a rundown hotel to give her $100 multiple times to make sure she was okay.

In order for me to do business with this girl, I had to meet her where she was at. I had to give her what she asked for from me, or she was going to pull the plug on the whole deal we had already worked out. Most people are not willing to even talk to these kinds of people.

These are some of the untold stories of professional real estate wholesalers. Because you're dealing with distressed, motivated people who have problems, you get yourself into some very strange situations sometimes. The people you're working with are people who often times have made a lot of bad decisions.

And you're the one who is stepping in to help them solve their problems. This is very tough for some people. Many people can't deal with all the headaches involved, so they give up.

To be successful in this business, you have to be calm, understanding and helpful to the people you're dealing with. I've been in some situations where I've had to get contracts signed on the side of the road with people who looked like they were about to beat me up.

The honest truth is if you want to be successful in this business, you're going to have to do things you don't feel comfortable with. You're going to have to get out of your comfort zone, and you're going to have to get comfortable with being uncomfortable.

And being uncomfortable doesn't just apply to dealing with the homeowners. It applies to working with investors, too. You have to be willing to put yourself out there and risk being told no. Not everyone can handle being told no. Some people get told no once, and then they quit. They decide this business isn't for them, and I'll be honest—it's not for everyone, and it can be especially tough in the beginning.

At first, when you're pitching your deals to investors, they aren't going to know who you are. They aren't going to trust you. Most of the time, they're going to think you're a flake. My advice to you if you're just getting started is you have to actually know what a deal looks like.

This is a problem I see a lot of other wholesalers have. They pitch a deal to me, but it's not a deal. They want me to buy something that's full retail or more. They don't know their numbers.

If you're trying to become a wholesaler, know your numbers. Make sure there is a lot of equity in the deal, and don't overcharge. If you're overcharging for your deals, you're not creating value for your investors. And if you're not creating value for your investors, then they're not going to buy from you. It's as simple as that.

Investors who want to buy deals are not idiots. They have cash. They know what a deal looks like. If you can bring them a deal where they can capture lots of equity for a small fee, they'll love you. They'll think you walk on water.

When I was just getting started, I made deals with investors where I walked away only having made $500. But in the beginning, this is the price you have to pay to build a relationship sometimes.

This business is built on quantity, not quality. Quality does matter as you progress, but sometimes you have to take what you can get. If you try to sell a deal to an investor, and you try to get too much out of it, they're just going to walk away and never work with you again.

For example, let's say you want to make $5,000 on a deal, but an investor only wants to give you $1,000. You could just walk away, but then you'd end up losing in the long run.

It's better to just take the $1,000, and then give all the value and equity to the investor. If you do this, he's going to come back for more. He's going to want to buy a deal from you every month.

If you can get 10 or 12 guys wanting to buy a deal from you every single month, you're set. You don't have to hit a home run on every single deal. A single investor who returns to buy from you month after month is worth a lot more money than any one deal is ever going make you.

A lot of wholesalers don't understand this concept. They get greedy, and they try to make $20,000 on every deal. But if you want to do wholesaling the right way, you need to learn to give and take. Would you rather make $20k once and your investor not happy or $5-10k every other month and establish relationship long term so he's consistently buying your deals?

Once you've built a relationship with an investor, and you've given them a lot of value and equity, over time you can start scaling up and charging them more for your deals because you've already provided them with a great service they trust. They will have grown to like working with you, and they won't mind paying the fees you ask them for. It is all about building the relationship and providing value as a wholesaler.

Skills Get the Deals

Wholesaling real estate is a game of patience. When you are dealing with people who are in distress, a lot of strange things can happen. You have to be understanding, helpful, empathic and willing to do whatever it takes to make a deal go through. When you're dealing with investors, you have to be willing to give them value in the beginning to build a relationship with them. You can't expect to hit a home run on every deal it's all about providing value and making the deal a win/win for the homeowner, investor and yourself.

Chapter 9

Find a Niche Market

I see a lot of people trying to wholesale real estate in large markets, and they're struggling. This is why I always tell my students they should work in smaller markets the big fish haven't gotten to yet.

It's always best to find a niche market, and then you can become the go-to guy in that market. The key component to dominating the niche market you've chosen to work in is you've got to have a marketing budget. You have to have some money available in order for you to get your name out there. You have to do everything you can to get all the leads coming to you before anyone else can get to them.

When you have the cash available to fund a marketing budget ,then you need to focus on speed. If you can gauge the motivation of a lead that comes in on the phone, stop everything you're doing and go meet with that lead. Don't put any time between that phone call and the meeting. In this game, speed kills.

I don't care how busy you are. If you know the deal is good, go meet with the lead right away. Being aggressive and working fast is how I've come to dominate my market. To put it simply, I get to the deals before everybody else.

Every realtor and flipper in my town is always telling me, "Chris, please start sharing some of your deals." To me, this is just a sign that I'm doing good work. I likely get to 80 percent of the investment properties that come through Lafayette before anybody else even looks at them because I'm everywhere.

I've done my best to achieve omnipresence and branding in my market by putting up billboards, bandit signs and Facebook ads. I put ads in magazines, newspapers, and on social media. I hand out business cards at my kids' soccer games. I do everything I possibly can to get people to know who I am and what I do because I want to be in the mind of my market.

I was born and raised in my market, so a lot of people here already know me. I was already a successful business owner in this area before I started wholesaling real estate, so I was trusted when I got started. A lot of people already knew who I was and knew that I was legit.

You may or may not have this advantage, so my advice to you is if you live in a small town, get people to know your name. Do everything you can to get your name and phone number out there, because that's how people are going to find you. You probably already have some relationships in place with people who can help you with this. Every small town has its key players and cash buyers, and you need to know them—more importantly, they need to know you.

If you're in a larger market, you have to get people to know your business. It's probably going to take a lot more money to do this. If you're in a big market, nobody cares about your name, so you don't have that advantage going for you. There's really no cookie-cutter system you can follow. But if you want less competition, smaller markets are the way to go. Big markets are extremely competitive, and they're generally dominated by major operations spending 20-40k a month, not guys who do this on their own.

The only thing that you have to do absolutely every time you do any type of marketing, no matter if you're in a big market or a small one, is split test different marketing channels. See what is getting you the best results and the best return on your money. Take a look at what's working in your specific market, and put more resources into that. If it's not working in your market, stop doing it. You have to make adjustments as you go. However, with whatever marketing channel you adopt you need to go deep and spend the money to see if it converts. You can't just buy 50 bandit signs and expect to see results. Try putting out 1,000 to see if that marketing channel converts. Same goes for any marketing channel you pick. If you are going to cold call, call 1000 people not 50! The point is split test and go deep to see what happens.

I'll give you an example. A while back, I did a Facebook video ad of me in my back yard by my pool talking about what I do as a wholesaler. I hit all the pain points. I talked about how I could help get people out of bad situations where they have to sell their homes fast.

When I ran this ad in Lafayette, it did amazing. The ad was costing me about 800 bucks a month, but I was making around $20,000 a month off of it. So, what I decided to do was take that same exact ad and run it in Baton Rouge where nobody knows me. It didn't work. It didn't get me a single lead, because nobody knows me in Baton Rouge.

It is very difficult to get people to know you everywhere. However, I would say it is going to be easier to get the business start in a market that people already know who you are. Furthermore, I would say the best markets to wholesale in are middle American where the medium price range is $150,000.00 - $200,000.00 a house.

If you have no marketing budget or a very small one, your biggest asset is your mouth. You must tell everybody what you do. You can use social media to do this, but you also have to do this in person everywhere you go like I told you I do. You can't be shy.

You don't even have to have a business page to promote yourself on social media. Facebook allows you to have 5,000 friends. So, what you can do is find people you're already friends with in your area, and then find their friends who live near you also, and add them until you're maxed out.

Then you can just post on your personal page on social media, and your message has a chance of being seen by the right people in your area. At least once per day, you can put a post up about how you buy houses. It doesn't even matter if you even get one like.

You're not trying to win a popularity contest. You're trying to get into people's minds. You want them to see what you do. If you do this over a sustained period of time, when people think of you, they'll think of what you do. Then they'll send someone to you who needs help, or they'll ask you for help themselves.

If you really want to wholesale real estate, and you have people skills, there's no reason you can't find deals without spending a lot of money on marketing. It's going to take more work, but once you get that first deal, you can roll that money into your marketing budget. Just remember, if at all possible, start with a small, niche market, and then expand from there.

Skills Get the Deals

Find a niche market to work in, and totally dominate that market, C and D markets are much better markets to wholesale in then A and B markets. Larger markets are full of much more competition. But you don't need to work in a huge area to make a lot of money. Having a marketing budget and focusing everything you put out on a specific area will get you the best results. If you have no budget, your biggest asset is your mouth and your social media account. Tell everyone what you do. Get them to put your name with the fact that you buy houses. Over time, this will brand you into their minds. When you start to make money, roll it into your marketing budget, and keep momentum moving in your favor.

Chapter 10

You Need Energy and Enthusiasm

As a kid, I had so much energy and enthusiasm that they labeled me ADD and ADHD. They put me on medicine when I was nine years old, and it almost ruined my life. It made me anti-social, and it drained the life right out of me.

Because of my experiences growing up, I'm now a huge anti-drug advocate. I would never put any kid on any kind of psychotropic drug. It just kills their spirit.

Kids and adults who are full of energy don't need to be changed. They are fine just the way they are. They don't need to conform to the way the school system thinks they should be. They just need to find a way to channel their energy into something positive and productive. They just need their energy to be redirected.

If you take a look at the most successful people in the world, they typically weren't straight A students. Look at Bill Gates and Steve Jobs. They didn't even finish college, and now they're household names. I'm in no way comparing myself to them, but when people say, "If you don't make straight As, and you don't sit still in class, you're not going to be successful," that's just not true.

If you happen to be reading this, and somebody told you that when you were growing up, welcome to the club. I grew up being told that all of my life. But what I've found out now that I'm older is that just because you're wired differently doesn't mean you can't be successful.

In fact, I believe that in this industry, if you have more energy than other people, that's actually a gift. I have so much energy that I can work for 12 to 14 hours a day like it's nothing. I can work Monday through Sunday and not ever get tired of it. I'm like a machine, and I love every minute of it.

Sometimes my wife has to tell me, "Dude, you need to put it down." But I like to be creative. I like to do productive things, be on the go and keep my energy up. When I was growing up, that didn't always work out well for me in the school environment. I was lucky to have a mother who supported me through it all and told me all the time that I was capable of doing big things.

Once I got out of school, I thrived. In the real world of business and entrepreneurship, you have to be on the move. If you're not, then somebody else is going to beat you to your next deal. The real world won't hold you back. Because in the real world time is money, and speed kills.

When it comes to the wholesale real estate business, the guys who are quiet and low energy are the ones who fail. And the guys who aren't afraid to talk to people and have a lot of energy to go and meet with all different kinds of people are the ones who succeed. I've seen that this is true with students time and time again.

When I started taking ADD medicine when I was nine, it just zombified me. It killed my creativity. My personality and energy went away, and I felt numb. I was always irritable. I could barely sleep because all of the medicine is essentially legal meth. I could barely eat when I took it. But I didn't associate any of the problems I was having with the pills I was taking, because I was too young to know that was even a possibility.

I took the pills all throughout high school, and I knew I wasn't myself. I made bad decisions I don't think I would have made otherwise. I started dabbling in drugs. I got caught up in cocaine, ecstasy and partying. Combined with taking Adderall and Ritalin everyday, the things I was doing resulted in me developing an addictive personality. My life from the age of 18 to 22 was not going well, and I knew I was messing up.

So, I sought out help. I completed a 23-day detox program, and when I got out, I never touched another drug again. I remember feeling like I had been restored back to life.

As soon as I came out of the purification program, I dived deep into personal development. I started reading a book every week. I started absorbing teachings from people that I admired. My main drive was I wanted to become a better version of myself. I can attribute most of my success in business to this drive.

If you want to be a successful real estate wholesaler and real estate investor like I am, or you just want to be a successful in general, this is where your success begins. You have to constantly work on bettering yourself.

Shortly after I got out of the detox program and started studying personal development, I started my own on-site oil change, car wash and auto glass business. I started making great money, and my wife and I built our first home. We sold it five years later, because people were leaving New Orleans to move into our area of Louisiana following Hurricane Katrina in 2005.

The hurricane caused the demand for houses in our area to soar, and home prices in our area doubled pretty much overnight. When we sold our home, we made $125,000 on it, and that was when I got my first taste of how much money could be made in real estate.

In my life, I believe one of the reasons I've been successful is because I visualize what I want, and I believe I'm going to get it. This is something I learned to do when I first began studying personal development. My wife and I have been writing down our goals since we were 22 years old, and every single one of the goals we've written down we've accomplished.

For example, at the time of this writing, we're buying a million-dollar beach house in Destin, Florida that we wrote down that we wanted when we were 24. Working with Grant Cardone is another goal I wrote down, and I told my wife I wanted to be in his space. Now we're 10X Growth Conference sponsors for real estate wholesaling.

I can give you more examples of how this simple process of writing goals down has worked for me. My wife and I have always wanted to own acreage in a place called Youngsville, Louisiana. It's a beautiful, highly desirable place to live, but it's very hard to find property there because it's so expensive, and it doesn't become available very often.

Because we knew we wanted this property, my wife wrote down for one of our goals, "We will find acreage to build our dream home in Youngsville." The next day, a realtor called us, and we bought 15 acres in Youngsville for half price.

Part of the property we're going to use to build a home on, and the other part we are developing commercially. When it's all said and done, we will make money on the property itself, and we will have the home of our dreams. All of this came about because five months before, my wife wrote on her Facebook page, "We're looking for property in central Youngsville."

All of these examples are proof that you have to know what you want, and you have to ask for it. You don't have to believe other people who have told you that what you want is impossible. You don't have to believe other people who have told you that you're never going to be successful.

If you're like me, and you have a lot of energy, you can put it to good use by writing down your goals and seeing them through. You may not believe me right now, but what I've found is that when you get clear about what you want, the universe will find a way to bring it to you.

Skills Get the Deals

I grew up knowing I was wired differently. I was labeled ADD and ADHD at a young age, and I was put on drugs to make me more like the school system thought I needed to be. But what I've found is that people who are successful in wholesaling real estate are high energy, just like I am. They aren't afraid to talk to people, and they love to work in a fast-paced environment. I've learned over time to channel my energy into productive goals. The best way to do this is to start by writing your goals down. Then work towards them every single day, and I guarantee you will be surprised with the results.

Chapter 11

Be a Great Communicator

The biggest thing my students love about me is the service I give them. My students are able to talk to me every single day if they want to. There's no wholesale real estate coach in this country that provides this level of service. My students are super successful because wholesaling real estate is a situational business, and I give my students advice specific to whatever they're going through.

I help my students with their specific problems. I don't just give them cookie-cutter advice and expect them to read between the lines. I've been in the game for a while now, and I know that things can get out of hand really fast.

This is why when my students have an issue, they can call me and say, "Hey, Chris, I don't know how to handle this situation. What should I do?" When I get their message, I shoot them a message right back, and I don't waste time getting to the point. I tell them exactly what they need to do.

This type of accessibility and service is what makes my coaching service stand out. This is what makes me different. But for you, the wholesaler, this same concept of how I provide service to my students applies to how you should be conducting all aspects of your business.

People who are in distress don't want to talk to a non-emotional entity such as an automated phone system. They want to deal with somebody who is understanding, caring and loving. They want to deal with someone who cares about their situation and wants to help them, someone who is real.

If you can be accessible to people, and allow them to speak their minds, that's how you can close deals. You have to become a listener, because motivated sellers are motivated for a reason. They have a huge problem in their life, and as we all know, people with problems love to talk about them.

But people who are willing to listen to people with problems are rare. Most of the time, people are too caught up in their own to ever both to listen to anybody else's.

I see a lot of people come into this business, and they want to automate all kinds of things right away. They spend a lot of money on high-end gadgets and gizmos that send messages out for them, and in my opinion these things are just not worth spending money on. I'm telling you right now, I go against the grain, and I dominate the wholesale game in my area primarily because I pick up the phone, and I listen to people tell me about their problems.

Of course, it's a little more complicated than that. I have to guide the conversation in a certain way, and there are certain things I'm listening for when people are telling me their problems. I have to filter out the people who have a situation I can help them with from the people who have a situation I can't help them with.

I have to do what's known as qualifying the lead. For a lead to qualify to work with me, the first thing I need to know is if they have enough equity in their home to sell it at a price that allows me to make money when I sell it to an investor. Second, they have to have a decent location. If a property is way out in the boondocks, and it's not a desirable property I can flip, wholesale or rent out, then I don't want to mess around with it.

You can imagine how difficult it sometimes is to actually get this information. You have to go about finding out this information in the right way, otherwise you risk making people really mad at you. You have to remember you are working with people who are generally in a very unbalanced emotional state, and you don't want to say something that might trigger them.

Being able to talk to people the right way so that they feel taken care while you get the information you need is the secret to success in this business. You have to have people skills to accomplish this. You have to actually care about people, and you have to be there for them when they need you.

I see people in Facebook groups I'm a part of talking all the time about the newest technology that sends messages for you and this and that, just pick up the phone and talk to people. It's never going to be a true substitute for an understanding ear.

The one thing that you should focus on as a wholesaler is talking to buyers and sellers. This is what is going to make you money, so it's what you need to focus on.

This doesn't mean you can't hire anybody else to work for you. I've had a personal assistant since I was 24, and she's helped me by taking care of a lot of the administrative side of things for me.

If you want to be successful in this business, the most important thing you need to focus on is becoming a great communicator. To do that, like I said in the last chapter, you must become comfortable with being uncomfortable. Even to this day, I'm still pushing myself in this area. I still get uncomfortable sometimes. Sometimes weird things you could never predict happen, but the difference between me and someone who is just starting out is I don't let being uncomfortable stop me from getting done what needs to get done.

This is the best attitude you can have. And you can apply it to a lot of different areas of your business. I'll give you an example. Before I hooked up with Grant Cardone, I'd never been on TV. I'd never been on camera, and I had anxiety about it. But now that I have my own show with Cardone, I've seen that those fears I had about being on TV were just imagined. I get better at it every single time I go on, and the discomfort I felt about it originally has faded into the background.

To develop better communication skills, you don't have to reinvent the wheel. What you can do is find people who are great communicators, and then mimic them. Watch their mannerisms, pay attention to the inflections and cadences they use, and practice speaking just like they do.

To give you an example, one of my favorite speakers is a guy named Brian Tracy. When I wanted to get better at speaking on camera, I watched some of his videos online, and I practiced speaking like he does.

But having good communication skills isn't just about how you speak and what you look like when you speak. Learning simply to speak less and listen more, especially in this business, can go a very long way. Most people have a problem with being a truly good listener. Ask yourself right now, when you have a conversation with someone, do you really listen, or do you just wait to speak?

People, especially those in distress, can sense when you're not listening. They can tell when you're just waiting for your turn to talk. Becoming a good listener is just as much a part of the cycle of good communication as is being able to express yourself. Pretend the person you are talking to is someone you grew up with and played t-ball with.

And finally, there are certain things you can do that will make you more approachable to the people you come into contact with as a wholesaler. Your image is important. My students ask me all the time, "Should I dress in a suit? Should I wear a tie when I go meet with people?"

And I always tell them, "Absolutely not!" Let me tell you why: the people who you're speaking with who are in distress do not want to deal with corporate America. These people are stressed out. They're at their wits end. They've probably been dealing with lawyers or the bank or people like that, and the last thing they want to do is talk to somebody who looks like they want to get more money out of them.

If someone is going through pre-foreclosure, a divorce, or anything traumatic, they don't want to be intimidated by somebody in a suit and tie. They want to talk to somebody they can relate to, the guy next door.

You don't want to look like you just crawled out of bed, but you don't want to look like you're just there to sell them something. That's not the kind of person these people want to deal with.

If you can present yourself as someone who is relatable and cares, you will do a lot better in bridging the gap between you, your lead and the deal. To present yourself well, you have to be a great communicator.

Just remember "Skills get the deals"! You've got to be a people person. If you're not a people person, that's okay. This is something I can help you with in my training. We work on different skill sets like rapport building, being a good listener, negotiating, estimating repair cost, valuations and other things you need to know to become successful in this business.

Skills Get the Deals

The first step to great communication in any business is just making yourself accessible. Don't try to hide behind automation. To become a great communicator, watch people who you think are great communicators, and duplicate their approach. You don't have to reinvent the wheel. Being a caring and loving person goes a long way when you're working with people in distress. Be relatable because the people you're working with don't want to deal with anyone who is just trying to sell them something. Meet people where they're at, listen instead of just waiting to talk, and your efforts will go a long way towards helping you close deals and make money.

Chapter 12

Hard Work = Good Luck

One of the biggest mistakes I've made in business is being too trusting of other people. There have been times when I've not done my due diligence when it comes to a few particular people, and they've burned me.

What happened was I started making a lot of money, and people in my town started to find out how much money I was making. Then they started to gravitate towards me with all of their bad "moneymaking" ideas.

This happens to everyone who becomes successful. As soon as people find out you have money, they want a piece of you. People start to come out of the woodwork, and they seem to have all of these genius ideas.

My problem was I wasn't careful. I didn't do my homework. I wanted to be nice to these people, and I honestly wanted to help them. But when it comes to business, you have to know who you're working with.

When you go into business with somebody, it's kind of like marrying them. When you marry somebody, everything might be great relationship wise while the finances are separate. But then when you start sharing the same money, things can get out of hand very fast. People have tons of relationship problems related to money.

The same goes for business. When you get into business with somebody, you might not know much about them. They might seem like a great person to work with until there's money involved.

Once you have money, other people are going to want it. It's just a fact. But you can't just give it out. You have to be smart and treat the people who are coming to you as if you are the bank, and they're trying to get a loan.

A bank doesn't just loan out money. They get to know everything about a person. When they're looking into giving a loan to someone, they look at how much money they make, if they've ever been arrested, and who their friends are.

If you're going to invest your money with someone, go ask five people who know the person you're considering investing with what they think of that person. I learned this lesson the hard way.

There have been three different instances where I've been burned for a total of $160,000. And if I had vetted the people who took advantage of me, I would have found out the truth.

Just because someone is nice to you in person does not mean they're a good person. Blind trust is never a good thing to have when it comes to handing over your hard-earned money. You can't just go off of your emotions and what feels right.

You can't make emotional decisions when it comes to any aspect of the business. You have to make logical decisions that you've thought through completely. This is why people who are sitting on hundreds of millions of dollars usually tell people who come to them for investments "no" 20 times before they say "yes" to anyone.

People often get caught up in get-rich-quick schemes thinking they can make easy money. But nothing is easy. You've got to work your ass off at anything in order to make money. The harder you work, the luckier you will get.

Sometimes people tell me, "Dude, you're so lucky," but that's not true. I create my own luck. And I create it by working extremely hard and following in the footsteps of people who are very successful.

In a very real sense, I'm not lucky because all I've done are things that anyone can do. The difference is that most people are not willing to do the things required of them to become successful, and I am.

If you're just getting started in the wholesaling business, the first thing I always recommend is that you hire a coach. Learn from them. Become them. If you don't have the money to hire a coach, the easiest and cheapest way to learn and grow is to read books.

When you read books written by people who are successful, you pick up some of their attributes. Personalities are changeable. They are moldable, but a lot of people don't think this. They think they are who they are, but this isn't true. You can change, and you can become like other successful people if you want to.

You can mold your personality to be more like the people you are studying, reading about and being mentored by. When you do this, you begin to realize that it's very easy to become successful. All you have to do is follow other successful people, and do what they say.

I've been very successful with what I do, and I still have mentors I model myself after. Grant Cardone is a huge mentor for me. The more I follow him and read his books, the more I am inspired to do big things and have a 10x mindset and become the best version of myself.

It's like when you're young, and you try to mimic superheroes. But the superheroes in your life now should be entrepreneurs who are doing what you want to do and absolutely crushing it. Those are the people you should look up to, follow and try to duplicate their actions.

Wholesaling real estate is a fantastic way to become an entrepreneur. Cardone told me once, "If I was 30 years old and just starting in real estate investing, this is what I'd be doing." Why did he say this?

Well, there are the least barriers to entry. You can start a real estate wholesaling business with little money, and you can turn that into millions within a few years.

If you look at some other avenues of entrepreneurship, like owning a franchise, you have to spend six figures just to get started. Even after you do that, you're still not even guaranteed to make money. If it doesn't work out, you're out of money, and on top of that you're probably stuck with a bunch of equipment you can't even use anymore.

But if you start a real estate wholesaling business, you're not tied down by it in any way. You're never going to get stuck with a house you can't sell, because when you create your contract, you make it so if you can't find an investor to buy the contract, you're not liable to pay for it either.

Wholesaling real estate is the least risky path to entrepreneurship I know of, and it's a path that can have you earning five figures a month in a relatively short amount of time. Not everyone is meant to do it, but if you've read this far into this book, and you're still not turned off by the idea, then there's a good chance you have what it takes to be successful with it.

And if it does work out for you, and you start making a lot of money doing it, then you really become powerful because you have access to a lot of deals to use to your financial advantage in any way you see fit. You become the source of the deal, and there's no greater position than that to be in.

Wholesaling real estate is truly a way to build generational wealth. My operation is very small. It's tight nit, and there are not a lot of moving parts. It's a very niche business, and the profits are enormous.

When someone calls us with a potential deal, I like to take the call sometimes because I want to be in the game. I want to be on the front lines for my business, because it keeps me sharp and in the know.

The same is true when it comes to my coaching business. I want to have direct contact with my students, and I take their calls because I know from experience that that's exactly what my students need in order for them to be successful.

There are a lot of wholesale real estate coaches out there who claim to teach what I teach, but I can guarantee that not one of them outworks me. Not one of them provides the level of service that I provide to my students.

Providing the best service to my students is what keeps me going. Seeing their success lights a fire in me and actually inspires me to want to keep growing my own wholesale real estate business.

I want to help a lot of people who don't come from money or didn't have a great upbringing break out of that cycle and start building generational wealth for their families. I have students who come to me when they're making $30,000 a year, and when they start to making $30,000 a month, it's like they've transformed into a whole new person.

I have students who are 19 years old who are focusing on wholesaling real estate, and they're going to be superstars one day because of their focus. So whatever you do from this point forward, I challenge you to focus.

Because it's so easy to start doing five different things, spread yourself too thin, and then end up getting nowhere with any of them. Having a coach to keep you focused and on the right path towards success can make all the difference.

There's a mentor of mine named Mark Evans DM, and he's one of the biggest real estate flippers in the country. I had a call with him, and I was telling him about a new venture I was going to begin.

And he told me, "Chris, whatever you do, you're going to be good at it. But you need to focus on one or two things, and do those really well. Because if you spread yourself too thin, you're never going to penetrate the marketplace."

It's like when you take a magnifying glass, and you put it in the sun, and you focus it on a leaf. It burns the leaf. But if you're moving the magnifying glass around, this doesn't happen and you burn nothing.

You have to give one hundred percent of your focus to wholesaling, and that's why I've become so successful at it. All of my attention is focused on how to make my business better, how to make my students' businesses better, how to close more deals, how to get more houses under contract, and how to get more investors on board with what I'm doing.

If you have the drive to succeed, don't let anybody hold you back. Put yourself out there. Take a chance, get in the game, and give it all the energy you've got. And if you decide you need help, I'm just a phone call away.

Skills Get the Deals

Don't ever make a decision to turn over your money to someone that you haven't completely vetted, Trust people but verify their actions. When you're making a business decision, remember to use logic and reason instead of basing your decision off of your emotions. If you want to be a successful entrepreneur, wholesaling real estate is one of the best possible ways you can get started. It doesn't require a lot of money, and the potential rewards are enormous.

Chapter 13

Connect Yourself to Power

I first discovered Grant Cardone a couple of years ago. I started reading his books because he's from a small town called Lake Charles that's about 45 minutes west of where I'm from. Then I started watching his YouTube videos, and the first thing I noticed was that he spoke with a passion and a fire that resonated with me.

A short time after I started watching his videos online, I heard about his event called 10X Growth Conference, and I called his office to buy a ticket. I was blown away when he answered the phone himself.

I bought the top-of-the-line ticket to the event because I wanted to be seated right up by the stage. It was a $10,000 ticket, and I bought two of them, so it cost me $20,000. But it was the best investment I've ever made in my life.

When I first walked into the building, I could tell something was very different about the atmosphere. The people there were not like most people you come into contact with in every day life. They were all hustlers and entrepreneurs.

I could tell the people there were people who eat, sleep and breath entrepreneurship, day in and day out. I could tell they were all there to learn something and become a better version of themselves. It was like I had walked into a church for entrepreneurs. It was an almost spiritual experience.

On the very first day, I got to hear Bobby Castro speak. He's the president and co-founder of Bankers Healthcare Group, and he's also a hecta-millionaire. He spoke about the idea of non-refundable minutes. Meaning, you're either investing every minute of your time into something productive, or you're wasting it. This really resonated with me, because when it comes to my business, I know how valuable every single minute truly is.

There were so many great speakers, and I learned a lot from every single one of them. But on the last day when Cardone spoke, that's when something crazy happened for me. He was up there presenting, and he had a whiteboard he was writing on during his talk, but he accidentally wrote on it with a permanent marker.

When he realized the mistake, he stopped, faced the crowd and said, "Well, now I'm going to have to sell this thing. Who wants it?"

I stood up and yelled in front of the whole crowd, "I want it!"

He said back, "Give me $3,000."

And I said, "You got it." I bought it right there on the spot because somehow I just knew this event was going to be life changing, and I wanted to take a piece of it home with me. A lot of the speakers at the event had written on that white board, and Cardone himself had written all over it while he was talking about how to create your ideal scene in life. I still have this board in my office to this day. I don't plan on ever getting rid of it.

Before I left the conference, I went into Cardone's office to buy Cardone U, which is his sales training program. I bought the program because if you bought it, then you got to book a meeting with him. I booked the very first meeting slot available with him the next morning in his office.

When I got to the meeting, he signed the white board I'd bought at the conference. Then I straight up asked him if he'd be interested in doing something with me in regards to real estate wholesaling. He said yes, and he typed something into his computer like "do something big with Chris Rood on wholesaling." After that, I got hooked up with his production manager Robert Sylso, and I got my own show on CardoneTV talking about wholesaling.

It was a huge step for me because I had to put myself on camera. I had never been on camera before, but I had to start creating content about how to wholesale real estate and sending it to his office. What I learned from doing this was that putting yourself on camera breaks you down and stretches you to grow in every way.

Once I started doing content for Cardone to give information to his audience, it totally blew up my business. Everybody in my town knew what I was doing. Not only did it help me with my coaching company, it also helped me with my wholesaling business because people started to trust me even more as a professional.

Once I connected myself to Cardone, I became one of the fastest growing real estate wholesaling coaches in the country. If I had tried to achieve this organically, it would have taken forever, and there's a chance that it might not have ever even happened. There's no way to predict how things are going to go when it comes to stuff like this.

But this is the key point I want to make in telling you all of this: one of the biggest things you can do to make your business blow up is connect yourself to power. There are so many examples of how this works in the real world.

I'll give you an example that everyone is familiar with—Dr. Phil. Nobody knew or cared who Dr. Phil was before he started working with Oprah. If he hadn't made that career move, people would still not know who he is. But because he connected himself to power, now he's a name that everybody knows.

But connecting yourself to power is not just about increasing your popularity. It's also about increasing your knowledge. It's about finding expert mentorship for yourself so you can start to play at the next level.

Everyone has mentors. Everyone has people who they learn from and connect themselves to in order to gain access to more opportunities. If you want to do well in the world of business, you have to get to know the people who make it turn on its axis.

Even Cardone has mentors, and his mentors are billionaires. It doesn't matter how far you make it in business, you can always learn more. You can always make more valuable connections that can benefit you in more ways than one.

When you connect yourself to power, the demands on your time and skills also increase, so you have to be prepared for that. You can't expect to get to the next level and not step up your game. That's not how it works. You have to prove yourself, and you have to show that you deserve to be there.

But if you have a connection to power, use it. It will take you where you want to go much faster than if you try to get there on your own. You don't have to wait for fate to make these connections for you. You can reach out to mentors who you'd like to work with, and get the ball rolling for yourself. So, hire a mentor and connect yourself to power!

Skills Get the Deals

When you connect yourself to power, you gain more visibility, more respect and more knowledge. On top of that, you also gain access to more opportunities, and people trust you more. You don't have to wait for the stars to align to make a connection with someone who is playing at the next level in business. Find out who the key players are that you resonate with, and then follow them. Take in all of their content and see if they offer some kind of mentorship program you can be a part of. Like I've said in previous chapters, business is all about building relationships, and one key relationship has the power to totally transform your business.

Chapter 14

Mindset and Conclusion

Mindset. What does this mean? The dictionary defines this term as: 1) An attitude, disposition, or mood. 2) An intention or inclination. You have to understand that this book is mostly about the mechanics of wholesaling real estate and not about the mindset needed to be successful in this business.

Marketing and the actions needed to start the business is all mechanics. This accounts for about 20% of the business. The other 80% is mindset.

What do I mean by mindset? Mindset is a broad subject, but I will keep it short and sweet. It's basically your internal belief system in regards to yourself and others. You've got to KNOW and BELIEVE you're going to be successful, not just THINK and HOPE! Do you see the difference?

If you just say to yourself, "Well, I'll just give it a try and see what happens," then you've already lost. If you don't

BELIEVE you're going to be successful, then don't get into this business.

Now, I'm not saying that if you just believe in yourself you will be successful. You will still hit roadblocks and barriers, and you will experience frustration regarding your marketing strategies and the business in general.

But what I mean to tell you is that you've got to have a no quit attitude and an intention to be successful that is so strong that nothing will change your mindset.

Visualize what you want! Write it down, and be very intentional about what you want. Know you deserve it wholeheartedly! Oh, and don't forget: SKILLS GET THE DEALS! Go get it!

Marketing Strategies for Different Time Vs. Money Situations

No Money, Lots of Time

- Driving for dollars
- Bandit signs
- Networking: realtors, contractors, subcontractors, roofers, AC companies, plumbers, divorce attorneys, bail bondsmen, mailmen, cops, firefighters, etc.
- Craigslist
- Leverage + post on social media
- Join REI groups
- Vehicle wraps
- Door knocking
- Expired listings

Money to Market, But No Time

- Create a heavy online presence, i.e. a website, SEO, PPC, and/or Facebook ads
- Newspaper articles
- Direct mail to a very targeted list
- Ringless voicemail i.e. Slydial

- Billboards
- Vehicle wraps
- Hire birddog/driving for dollars

Money to Market and Time

- Direct mail/post cards
- Bandit signs
- Online presence = SEO, PPC, and Facebook Ads
- Newspaper articles
- Set up cold calling office/do everything
- Slydial
- Billboards
- Network with realtors

Successful Wholesaler Traits

Why are some wholesalers successful and some not? I've studied both, and I can tell you why!

Traits to look for:

- Great communication skills (people skills). Skills get the deals!
- Great at sales
- Has a pleasing personality
- Really consistent with his/her follow up
- His/her hustle or speed of action (execution) is fast—this is very important.
- Really good at building rapport and establishing a relationship with the homeowner
- Consistent with marketing month in and month out
- Really loves people and truly cares about them
- Is a genuine person
- Visualizes their success before implementing plans
- Willing to take a risk
- Committed to personal development and always improving and working on sharpening skills
- Is very confident in his/herself
- Is very intentional about what he/she wants

- Is very ethical
- Thinks very highly of his/herself
- Knows his/her market inside and out
- Is highly competitive
- Knows what things cost to fix and can estimate repair cost

If you feel that you don't have any of these traits or you just have a few of them, that's okay. Just partner up with someone who does have them!

About Chris Rood Coaching

Online course teaching traditional wholesaling, lease option wholesaling, wholetailing, and buy and hold course on single family homes.

You'll get a one on one welcome call from me giving you the exact strategies I use to crush it in my market.

You will have access to our private Facebook group to ask whatever questions you need.

www.ChrisRood.com

Thank you for reading my book

Special thanks to Grant Cardone for all the help and for changing my business at 10X Growth Con.

"If I Was 30 Years Old & Just Starting In Real Estate Investing, This Is What I'd Be Doing. "

-GRANT CARDONE

Thirteen reasons why most people don't succeed in wholesaling

1. You don't know and understand your market.
2. You think all the deals are on MLS.... The best deals are direct to seller.
3. You don't know what things cost to fix.
4. You don't know how to buy right, you only control the buy so buy right!
5. You are not intentional with your offer.
6. You are scared to make lowball offers.
7. You don't connect with the homeowner.
8. You are scared to spend money on marketing.
9. You don't have the confidence in yourself and you are not certain of yourself.
10. Your follow up sucks.
11. Your people skills and likeability index are very low. Skills get the deals!!!
12. Your unwillingness to network and put yourself out there is cowardly.
13. You are scared to build relationships with your buyers and you fail to understand what your buyers are looking for and want.

<u>Books I recommend everyone to read</u>

For mindset

1. The Science of Getting Rich
2. The Strangest secret
3. Think and Grow Rich
4. 12 Pillars
5. Listen to your wish is your command series on YouTube by Kevin Trudeau

On discipline, action, and consistency
1. The Compound Effect
2. The Slight Edge
3. The 10x Rule
4. The One Thing

On Communication Skills

1. Everyone Communicates but Few Connect
2. Never Split the Difference

On Systems

1. Traction
2. E-Myth

Datalist: Listsource.com

Robogateway.com

Propertyradar.com

Attomdata.com

Call porter for direct mail answering service

Skiptrace: needtoskip.com

TLO

IDI

Lexus Nexis

Cold Call Company: 1000 calls a day

Skip tracing done for you: Rei market pro

Data zap

Ringless voicemail: Stratics Network

Slydail

Skippo

Ringless Broadcast: Message communication

text blast

Website: Investor Carrot

Adword nerds

SEO Chief Marketing

Final Note

Understand that this book talks a lot about marketing strategies and the mechanics of wholesaling however, your ability to be an effective negotiator and communicator is ultimately going to make you or break you in this business. I suggest that after reading this book that you work on your people and negotiating skills if you want to crush wholesaling.

Stay tuned for my next book on negotiation and rapport building called Skills get the Deals.

<u>Leave A Legacy</u>

How do you want to be remembered by your kids and grandkids? How many of you want to leave some wealth to you kids and grandkids? I don't know of a better wat to leave a legacy to your family than by doing it through Real Estate Investing! If you start with wholesaling, you will have substantial increase the chances of that being a reality! Why is that?...... Because you'll become the "Source of the Deal"!! You will be in first position and you will have captured the most equity on these properties and you will have laid the foundation for your real estate business if you have the wholesaling piece in. The point is you need to go "direct to seller" to have the best chances of getting the best deals! Period! The only way to do that is to create a wholesaling business!

They do not teach this stuff in school. If they showed people how to find great Real Estate Investment properties using the wholesale method, people would generate wealth through real estate very quickly. Learn it, use it, generate cash and equity on properties and leave a legacy to your family!

Wealth Creation Formula

1.) Create Wholesale Business.

2.) Wholesale majority of the deals to stack cash.

3.) Only keep the best deals to flip that are in the best location that don't need a lot of work. Wholetail it if possible and stay in the sweet spot as far as price point in your market, my market's sweet spot is 150-200K and below. If you do this and it doesn't sell you could still rent it out or sale it on a lease option or owner finance. Regardless if it doesn't sell and you bought it at wholesale prices you could always give it away for super cheap and at least break even because you bought it right.

4.) Take all the cash you made and put it into the best buy and hold properties that come through your wholesale pipeline that are in the best rental areas.

5.) Upgrade into multifamily and commercial as you start getting more cash.

I have been a Real Estate Investor for 13 years. If I would have known about the wholesale aspect of this business when I first got started I would be 10x further along than I am now and be worth 10x more. Get into Real Estate! Start with wholesaling! Go direct to seller and become
"The Source Of The Deal"

89943524R00064

Made in the USA
Middletown, DE
19 September 2018